LEARNING COMMUNITIES

Sara Connolly

University of Bridgeport

PEARSON

Prentice
Hall

Upper Saddle River, New Jersey
Columbus, Ohio

Vice President and Publisher: Jeffery W. Johnston
Executive Editor: Sande Johnson
Editorial Assistant: Lynda Cramer
Production Editor: Alexandrina Benedicto Wolf
Design Coordinator: Diane C. Lorenzo
Cover Designer: Candace Rowley
Cover Photo: Fotosearch
Production Manager: Pamela D. Bennett
Director of Marketing: David Gesell
Marketing Manager: Amy Judd

This book was set in Times Roman by Prentice Hall. It was printed and bound by Command Web. The cover was printed by Phoenix Color Corp.

Pearson Education Ltd.
Pearson Education Singapore Pte. Ltd.
Pearson Education Canada, Ltd.
Pearson Education–Japan

Pearson Education Australia Pty. Limited
Pearson Education North Asia Ltd.
Pearson Educación de Mexico, S.A. de C.V.
Pearson Education Malaysia Pte. Ltd.

10 9 8 7 6 5 4 3 2 1
ISBN 0-13-232243-9

CONTENTS

Note: Every effort has been made to provide accurate and current Internet information in this booklet. However, the Internet and information on it are currently changing, so it is inevitable that some of the Internet addresses listed in this text will change.

PREFACE

This booklet provides an overview of learning communities in colleges and universities. There are many good resources on learning communities, but very few are geared toward students. This booklet is intended for first-year college students and includes relevant examples and information from their peers. You will find real-life examples from community colleges as well as four-year colleges that illustrate the four types/models of learning communities. You will also find profiles of students who actually participated in learning communities. These students believe that their involvement in their learning community led them to other great opportunities. I found that both the students and the faculty are enthusiastic about learning communities and the possibilities that they offer.

■ ACKNOWLEDGMENTS

Thank you to all of the colleges and universities, and their representatives, who were more than willing to provide information about their learning communities, particularly: Dan Bivona at Arizona State University; Casey Blanton at Daytona Beach Community College, Florida; Alice Earp and Karen Laughlin at Florida State University; Heather Holmes at Salisbury University, Maryland; Sandra Hurd at Syracuse University, New York; Kami Mattson at The University of Wisconsin Marshfield/Wood County; Sue Mooney at Stonehill College, Massachusetts; and Sue Parsons at Cerritos College, California.

Thank you to the students who were willing to share their collegiate experiences and valuable advice with me and the world: Katie Riordan, Lauren Thomas, and Eddie Stankiewicz.

My thanks to the following reviewers who provided invaluable input: Robert J. Anderson at The College of New Jersey; Randolph Handel at Sante Fe Community College, Florida; Heather Holmes at Salisbury University, Maryland; Jacqueline Newcomb at Brown University, Rhode Island; and Beatrice Zamora-Aguilar at Southwestern Community College, California.

Thank you to all my wonderful friends and colleagues in higher education who helped me from outline to final version—this text is complete because of their input.

Last, but not least, thank you to my husband Pat for all his patience and assistance in reading and rereading the manuscript.

Sara Connolly

LEARNING COMMUNITIES

INTRODUCTION

Do you sometimes feel that the material you are learning in your college courses are irrelevant to what you want to major in or the career you want to pursue? Do you ever feel disconnected from your classmates and peers? Are you satisfied with the way you learn in your college classroom? As you begin your journey in college you may be feeling some of these fears—or some different ones—about what your college life will be like and whether or not you will succeed. You've probably heard that college could either be the best time of your life, the most difficult period of your life, or the time that you learn the most about yourself. Regardless, it will be a time that is different from anything you have experienced before.

MEET STEPHANIE

Stephanie is just completing her first year of college. She attends a large university, about five hours from home, in her home state. Stephanie was nervous about attending college. In her small high school Stephanie earned good grades, played a couple of sports, and took pictures for the high-school yearbook. Although she was eager to tackle the world of college, Stephanie was anxious that she wouldn't be able to get answers to her questions in the large classrooms that she envisioned. She also feared that it would be more challenging to have the close friendships that she had in high school.

When Stephanie was choosing her residence hall she carefully read through the literature sent to her home, as well as what was available on the college's website. She noticed that one option for her was a living/learning community, where she would live in a small residence hall and take one course, called a *colloquium*, with her hall mates. The literature noted that the class size would be limited to 25 students and—in addition to the colloquium—there would be trips to lectures, plays, and other activities specifically for the students in the community. Thinking that it sounded exactly like what she needed to ease her fears, Stephanie decided to apply. She wrote an essay and was accepted into the community. She is grateful to be in the community all year.

Many of her first year courses have over 200 students, but meeting with a faculty member in her colloquium class has given her the courage to seek out other professors during their office hours. She has made great friends in her hall and even plans to live off campus with some of them next year. The peer leader in her colloquium suggested that she try to work at the school paper, and she is now a staff photographer. Stephanie has enjoyed her first year of college and is excited about the challenges that her sophomore year will bring.

MEET LUKE

Luke is finishing his second semester of college with a 3.0 grade point average (GPA), and he is proud of the work that he has done this year. Although Luke worked very hard in high school, he was afraid that he wouldn't make it to college. Luke grew up in a poor community where few people went to college; in fact he is the first in his family to attend. His grades in math and science were always very good, but he needed some help in English and history, and his verbal SAT scores were not high enough. His school didn't offer honors or advanced placement courses, and he was afraid that this would also hurt his chances of getting into college. However, his high school guidance counselor was very supportive and she helped him fill out his college applications.

When a college about an hour away accepted him, he was really excited but was also nervous about the conditions of acceptance. Although the college saw potential in Luke, his SAT verbal score didn't meet their minimum requirements. So he would have to take a class the summer before his first semester to help him improve his writing skills. Luke was comfortable with this and eager to get a head start; however, the additional admissions stipulations concerned him.

The college also wanted him to take part in a special program, called a **_learning community_**, where students took four courses as a group. There would be a faculty member who worked with the group outside the classroom, as well as tutors and computer labs available to just the students in the learning community. Luke was afraid that being part of the leaning community would portray him as a remedial student, but he couldn't have been more wrong. All of Luke's classes included students from his learning community, from other learning communities, and from the general college population but no student was ever singled out.

The first semester was very challenging. It is sometimes overwhelming how much college professors expect from their students. Luke studies with his friends from the learning community a few nights a week, finds the learning community's computer lab really helpful (the one in the Union always has a long line), and has on several occasions taken advantage of the English tutors available to the community. Luke even found that his other friends often come to him for help now that he is doing so well in his classes. Luke now feels that he has the tools he needs to succeed in college. Although he does not plan to major in English, he no longer winces when a professor assigns a paper.

MEET CLAIRE

Claire is 20-years-old and is about to start school at a local community college. Claire didn't have the money to attend college when she was 18, so she took a few years after high school to work and save money. She has really enjoyed the time a 9 to 5 job has given her to spend with her family and her boyfriend, but she is also excited about going to college. After working in a pediatrician's office for two years she wants to become a nurse or a physician's assistant. She is confident that she will achieve those goals if she can just concentrate on college.

Her family and friends are all very supportive of her educational goals but they are used to her being around all the time to baby sit, attend family dinners, or go away for the weekend. She is concerned that she will be too distracted to concentrate on what she needs to learn.

She has started looking into the college's catalog and has noticed that, in addition to the classes for her intended biology major, she has to take a lot of other classes in other areas. She doesn't understand how English Composition and History of Ancient Civilizations can help her become a better nurse. Upon further research, she found that the college offers something that she finds interesting. The school has a **cohort** program: students in the cohort take the same classes together; meet with faculty members outside of the classroom together; and take courses based on a theme. Claire can choose Health Professions as her cohort.

Although she still has to take English and history, everyone in the class shares her concerns. They can help her gain a better understanding of how these courses can help her career ambition to be a health professional. She called the school and learned that the students in the cohort often earn very good grades and become extremely close. She thinks it might be just the thing to help keep her mind on school and help her understand how all the courses fit into what she wants to do. Claire is excited about attending the college and thinks that the sky is the limit for her potential within the learning community.

College is tough, and not everyone makes it to graduation. In fact, half of the students leave college before they graduate. This is a startling fact to students, faculty, and parents. Research has shown that the majority of students who drop out of college do so within their first year. In fact, over 50% of all institutional attrition occurs within the first year of school. Additionally, most of the students who leave college are choosing to do so. Although approximately 25% of the students who drop out within the first year are academically dismissed, 75% of students who leave are in good academic standing. Because only half of the students who start school stay to finish college, and those who leave do so in their first year, it makes sense that colleges and universities are spending a lot of time, effort, and money on programs that help students succeed during their first year.

Colleges have various programs designed to help you earn good grades, stay enrolled, and make you want to stay. The course that you are taking is an example of this type of programming, as are student activities and academic advising. As the stories of Stephanie, Luke, and Claire show, *learning communities* help increase your likelihood of success in college.

■ OBJECTIVES

After reading this booklet you should be able to confidently answer the following questions:

1. What is a learning community on a college campus?
2. Why do schools offer learning communities?
3. What are the different types of learning communities in higher education?
4. Why would I want to participate in a learning community?
5. How does a student get involved in a learning community?

WHAT ARE LEARNING COMMUNITIES?

There are many forms of learning communities—and the programs vary from campus to campus—but the basic tenet is the same across higher education. Students are enrolled in a set of common courses—oftentimes built around a theme—ranging from two classes to a full-semester load as a group or cohort. Hundreds of college campuses are now using learning communities. Although the programs offered vary among campuses, their goals remain the same.

■ GOALS OF LEARNING COMMUNITIES

Over the past twenty years, colleges and universities have been offering learning communities at increasing rates. While there isn't one individual reason for their use, the reasons revolve around a few themes.

1. **Increase Student Retention and Connection:** Includes interaction between faculty and students and among students

2. **Promote Student Leadership**

3. **Increase the Success Rate of Underrepresented Students**

4. **Integrate Classes Taken Across Disciplines and Improve Students' Critical Thinking Skills**

5. **Increase Student Learning and Achievement**

Increase Student Retention and Connection

Beginning a new life at a new school presents many challenges and can be overwhelming at times. However, college faculty and administrators are focusing more and more on what is needed to help you succeed and earn your diploma.

Over the past decades, numerous research have been conducted on the reasons students leave college before receiving their degree.

In the 1970's a researcher named Vince Tinto looked at the reasons students leave college.[1] His theory is that when students don't feel at home in college, socially and academically, they will likely leave. He based his theory on two measures: *academic and social integration.*

Academic integration, as you might guess, centers on classes and grades. When students are overly challenged, or not challenged enough, they tend to leave college early. This is not to say that you will not find some of your classes less (or more) challenging than others: each of your classes will challenge you in different ways. However, if you find that your classes are much easier than you expected, or that the classes are so hard that they are overwhelming, you are more likely to leave. If you cannot make the connection as to how your classes will help you in your career, you may also leave. While some students transfer to another college where they perceive the academic culture as a better fit, most never return.

Social integration focuses on college life outside the classroom. Tinto argued that this may be a more important factor than academic integration in a student's decision to leave. When you think about the amount of time you spend outside of class, this probably does not surprise you. The basic argument is that if you participate in campus activities, make a few friends on campus, and interact with faculty outside of class you are more likely to stay in school. These relationships help you feel more at home and, thus, make you more likely to stay. You may have noticed this in students in your residence halls or in your classes. The students who hang out in their room all day or go home every weekend are less happy with school than those who are make friends and find new things to do on campus.

If you decide to leave college it may ultimately be because you have not formed a connection to the school. Through learning communities and other programming efforts, colleges are trying to help you create that connection. During your college's orientation program you may have heard about the different ways to get involved on campus and were encouraged to do so as soon as possible. When you started school this fall, there were probably lots of clubs with tables set up in the Student Union. If you live on campus, the resident assistant on your floor may have encouraged you to attend floor meetings and get to know the other students in your residence hall better. These are all attempts to help you feel connected to your school. If you look a bit closer, you will likely find that there many opportunities that you could take advantage of. There is a club or organization for

---

[1]Tinto, V. (1993). *Leaving college: Rethinking the causes and cures of student attrition* (2nd ed.). Chicago, IL: University of Chicago Press.

different interests and groups, intramural sports, academic clubs, concerts, book clubs, and so much more.

Now we know that the majority of students who drop out do so during their first year, and that involvement in campus activities and interaction with faculty can help students stay. Therefore, it is logical that colleges would design programming that targets freshmen, encourages involvement on campus, and helps increase interaction between faculty members and students. Learning communities are designed to do just that—help you feel connected to the school, both academically and socially.

A study of learning community initiatives found that while 20% of schools indicated that their communities are an attempt to increase the retention rate, 39% said that they are to increase this connectedness through faculty–student and student-to-student interactions. Learning communities do have a significant impact on retention; however, their impact goes beyond keeping students in college until graduation.[2]

Promote Student Leadership

There are hundreds of books on leadership; many of those look specifically at leadership among college students and come up with varying definitions. It is likely that if you asked group of student leaders, each would have a different view of what it means to be one. For our purposes, we will characterize student leaders as possessing a set of attributes, which includes integrity, responsibility, sense of pride in their school, and civic duty to give back to the college community. Student leaders are generally involved in campus clubs and organizations, such as academic or social clubs, student government, sports clubs, and organizations based on race, ethnicity, and many others.

Student leaders are more likely to stay in school, perhaps because they are more involved on campus. They are also happier with the overall campus experience and earn better grades. Often, student leaders go on to become leaders in their community and their career.

Learning communities offer students the opportunity to become part of a community. They provide students with more opportunities to interact with other students and faculty members. Students are more willing to ask faculty members on how to join a club or develop an independent study if they interact with them

---

[2]Learning Communities National Resource Center,
http://www.evergreen.edu/washcenter/project.asp?pid=73

individually on a regular basis. In addition, students are more willing to seek out other students to join a club or organization, form a new group, or run for a position in student government due to the increased level of interaction. Students in learning communities talk to other students daily, attend study groups with them, and form relationships that go beyond the classroom.

In addition to all of these interaction opportunities, students in learning communities often have the ear of an upperclass student. Many learning communities have upperclass peer mentors as part of the program. The peer mentor provides insights into events and opportunities on campus that new students might not have known about otherwise. Additionally, students in learning communities often visit more areas of the campus than their peers through their study groups or colloquium classes, thus allowing them to see more of what resources are available.

As I am sure you already know, it isn't possible to force a student to become a student leader: the choice to become involved on campus or to become a student leader is up to each individual. However, the strength of learning communities is in providing opportunities that make it easier for students to become leaders.

Increase the Success Rate of Underrepresented Students

Although you have just begun your college journey, I'm sure you have already been asked what you intend to do with your degree or what job you would like to pursue after graduation. Even if you haven't thought about these, you have probably thought about how attending college can help you earn more money. College graduates generally earn, over their lifetime, salaries that far exceed those earned by people who have not attended college. College opens many doors of opportunity that would have otherwise not been accessible; hopefully your goal is to reap all the benefits that it offers. The opportunities that lie in front of you are now greater regardless of your background, race, ethnicity, and other factors.

However, this was not always the case. Many years after its inception, college was an opportunity only afforded to white men, thereby widening the gap between those who were able to further educate themselves and those who were not privy to such opportunities. Despite the fact that college is now accessible to a much broader population, there are still factors that contribute to a student's level of success. You may be the first in your family to go to college. Perhaps only a few people from your high school are attending college. Maybe you are starting school years after high school because college wasn't a viable opportunity for you then. Or you may belong to a minority group. Research has shown that students with these characteristics have a lower likelihood of success. They are least likely to finish college and tend to earn lower grades than their counterparts who have several generations of college graduates in their family.

Remember Luke and how nervous he was because he was the first of his friends and family to go to college. He turned to a learning community hoping that it would help him perform better. Being part of the learning community made him feel more confident about himself and the grades he was earning. Learning communities can help students from underrepresented groups to succeed in college and graduate. Recognizing that not all students learn in the same manner, learning communities provide opportunities for faculty and students to work together and find the best learning method that fits the students' needs. This is particularly advantageous to students who are unable to get advice from family members with previous college experience and for those who did not have a strong high-school curriculum.

Some learning communities are specifically designed for students with a weak background in a particular subject area, such as math, science, or English. There are also learning communities for students whose test scores were not at the level of general admission, but whose grade point average allowed them conditional acceptance. These learning communities offer courses in the necessary subject areas—often one level slightly below the standard college level—and allow the students to master the material. The learning community advisor counsels the students on their study habits and reading/test-taking techniques. Oftentimes, these learning communities also have study groups, computer labs, and tutors available for their members. A peer advisor (a successful upperclass student) with a similar background assists the students by demonstrating success and by giving them helpful tips on navigating through college.

Learning communities for underrepresented students help them find a community they are comfortable in; this allows them to seek assistance when needed and form long-lasting friendships with their peers.

Integrate Classes Taken Across Disciplines and Improve Students' Critical-Thinking Skills

Claire knew what she wanted to major in because she knew what career she wanted to pursue. However, she was not excited about the other classes that she had to take to earn her degree. Claire couldn't see how the classes outside her field of study would benefit her. However, participating in a learning community showed her how all the topics covered in the classroom gives her a well-rounded education and can, indeed, help her in her other classes. This was an important lesson for her and helped her feel more positive about college.

You may have already learned that college is more than learning a skill to do a job. If it were, you wouldn't need to spend several years earning your degree. College is also about maturing, learning to be a critical thinker, learning about cultures other than your own, finding out more about yourself, and so much more. The basic philosophy behind the liberal arts curriculum is that by taking a wide range of courses you train your mind to think critically. Once your mind has been trained you are more likely to become a lifelong learner, a more effective problem solver, and a better employee. Proponents of liberal arts education would argue that the skills to do a particular job can be easily taught to a person who has a well-disciplined mind.

There are many liberal arts colleges in America. If you attend one, much of your college curriculum will be composed of general liberal arts courses. Even if you do not attend a liberal arts college, chances are at least some part of your education will be in these courses. They are often referred to as basic studies courses, pre-requisite courses, general education requirements, or something similar. The basic tenet remains the same: taking a wide range of courses enables you to become a better critical thinker, a better problem solver, and well-educated in subjects beyond your specialty.

However, these benefits are not always achieved. Ernie Boyer, a higher-education professor who has completed a great amount of research on undergraduate education argued, in the 1980s, that there are two primary reasons for this.

1. Students do not generally come to college with the primary goal of becoming a critical thinker. Often, you are not attending college with the sole purpose of gaining a higher level of thought. More likely, you are attending college in order to gain a better career. You know that college graduates earn much more money over the long run than high-school graduates. You also know that you will have more career possibilities if you complete college. Therefore, you put up with your liberal arts courses, complain about them to your friends (you just know that you are never going to use the information gained in your World Civilizations class), and wait to finish all the important courses in your major.

2. Your professors, for the most part, think differently than you do. They have spent years researching and preparing for the classes that they teach. They are passionate about the material and think that you should be too. Additionally, the reward structure at colleges does not require teachers to win any popularity contests or have the most entertaining classrooms. Their job is to present the material to you. Your job is to absorb it. This lecture format,

which provides little interaction between students and faculty members, and the disjointed nature of these courses create a problem.

Because of these, students are not learning to process the material and integrate it to solve future problems. Faculty members become frustrated when students are unable to absorb their lecture and course materials and evaluate them critically. Businesses are frustrated when students cannot solve high-level problems creatively.

These frustrations and incongruous expectations are some of the major reasons why learning communities are formed. To quote one community-college professor who created learning communities on her campus,

> *We saw the traditional learning environment as reductionist and unrelated to real life. Creating a program where disciplines could come together was a way to emphasize a systems approach to learning and to knowledge.*

Communities, in addition to helping student retention by increasing their academic and social connections to the university, also help connect faculty and students to one another and to view the subject matter in new and important ways. They help both students and faculty members realize the importance of seeing other perspectives and integrating the course material into other disciplines. With some critical thought you will see how your world civilizations class provides you with important background information on cultures that will be useful in your psychology major.

Faculty members who teach in learning communities may incorporate some of this cross discipline perspective into their classroom content. Even if they don't provide this in their class lectures or assignments, learning communities provide opportunities for students to interact with faculty members more often on an informal level than they would in another classroom setting. These informal conversations often help the student see these perspectives. These new classrooms provide the further benefit of creating new spaces where students are no longer passive recipients of information and learn to integrate the knowledge they are gaining across disciplines.

Promote Student Learning and Achievement

Learning communities not only promote critical thinking in participating students, but also promote greater overall learning and better achievement, which are reflected in the students' grades. You are probably wondering how they can affect the entire college experience, and not just the learning community experience.

The argument is that students belonging to a community become better overall learners, and they then carry that knowledge and skill with them throughout their academic career. So far, all the arguments given for learning communities tie into student learning and achievement. After all, what is the point of becoming connected, integrating knowledge across disciplines, or staying in college if you are not learning while you are there?

In the 1980s in response to some of the problems that we just discussed—lack of integration of college material, lack of learning in the classroom, and student apathy—faculty and researchers developed the "Seven Principles of Good Practice in Higher Education."[3] True to its title, the document lists seven principles which faculty and administrators should follow in order to provide a high-quality experience for the students on their campuses. These principles are as follows:

1. Encourage contact between students and faculty

2. Develop reciprocity and cooperation among students

3. Encourage active learning

4. Give prompt feedback

5. Emphasize time on task

6. Communicate high expectations

7. Respect diverse talents and ways of learning

Learning communities address most, if not all, of these principles. Perhaps this is why most colleges and universities offer learning communities. In the section on student retention and connection, we talked at length about how learning communities attempt to increase contact between faculty and students and among students. Although learning communities are not the only way to increase this contact, they have certainly been proven as an effective method. In the next section, we will review what the research has to say about its effectiveness in this and other areas.

Learning communities help students discover their best way of learning and allow teachers to respond in the most effective way. As you may have experienced, traditional lecture halls do not allow for this personal interaction. Students become active learners in each of the learning community models. There are hundreds of ways students can participate in their own learning, but what is important is that learning communities allow students to be active participants.

---

[3]Chickering, A. & Gamson, Z. (Fall 1987). *Seven principles for good practice in higher education.* Washington Center News.

Moreover, faculty members are able to evaluate the student individually and continually give them feedback.

Learning communities are not perfect, nor are they the answer to all the problems in higher education. However, they do provide an opportunity to address several difficulties facing higher education today, including lack of interaction between faculty and students and among peers, lack of critical thought, and students who are not academically prepared for college-level work.

Some of the goals of learning communities, such as increasing student retention and achievement, are easily measured. Over time we can look at grades and graduation rates of students who participated in learning communities to see if they are successful. Other goals, such as increasing overall learning and student leadership, are harder to determine. Therefore, the important questions remain.

♦ Do they work?

♦ Are learning communities effective in delivering they set out to achieve?

IMPACT OF LEARNING COMMUNITIES

■ RESEARCH ON LEARNING COMMUNITIES

Learning communities cost money—both in real dollars and in human resources allocated to the programs. Researchers in higher education have been looking at learning communities for many years now. A great deal of research has been completed to evaluate their impact.

In case you are not well-versed in the types of research used in education, this section reviews some of the most popular methods. There are two major research categories: *evaluation* and *assessment.*

Evaluative research generally measures how well a project or program is received. Evaluative research in learning communities seeks to answer some of the following questions:

- ◆ Did the participants enjoy the experience?

- ◆ Did the participants receive what they anticipated from the experience?

- ◆ Was the experience valuable?

- ◆ What could (or not) be changed about the experience?

Assessment research involves evaluation but goes further to examine the impact of the program. In the case of learning communities, an overall assessment would include:

- ◆ Evaluating the program from all perspectives (student, faculty, administrators, and perhaps even family members)

- ◆ Measuring the impact of the community on other factors (such as retention, learning, and student involvement)

In order to assess a learning community, researchers use a variety of research methods. A researcher could use quantitative measures, which largely uses statistics, to determine impact.

Quantitative research can be used to examine the impact of the learning community on student retention from the first to the second year by comparing the retention rates to another group of non-participating students. In the real world it is not possible to remove all the variables that might confuse a cause-and-effect relationship. However, it is important that the researcher compares groups of students that are characteristically similar in other variables. In this example, the researcher could look at some of the background characteristics of the learning community group, such as race, family income, high-school grades and SAT scores, and education of parents. The researcher would then find a group of non-participants with similar traits. It is important to have similar groups in order to argue that the impact on retention is from participation in the learning community and not from another variable.

Qualitative research is another method used in educational research. Qualitative research is needed when the research question requires a more complex answer than a "yes-or-no" answer provides. This method is particularly helpful in understanding the depth of student learning that results from participating in a learning community as this effect is not easily measured. The qualitative researcher could review student journals or thesis, review written papers, observe classroom behavior, or interview students. He/she could evaluate the completed work of students in the program to determine the level of learning achieved, often using a pre-determined model of intellectual development. Papers from similar students who did not participate in the learning community would also be reviewed to determine differences. The researcher would also likely "test" learning at several points in the students' career by examining papers, conducting interviews, or using other research methods to determine differences between learning community participants and non-participants. Qualitative research is also useful in determining the community's long term impact on satisfaction, view of the college or university, and other perceived benefits.

The methods described above, and many others, have been used to determine the effectiveness of learning communities. Research results have shown that learning communities are worth the time and effort put into them. According to the Washington Center for the Improvement of Undergraduate Education, learning communities are effective.[4]

---

[4]http://www.evergreen.edu/washcenter/home.asp

■ INCREASED STUDENT RETENTION RATES

One of the major goals of learning communities is to increase the retention rate among sophomore college students. As you may recall, over half of the students who drop out of college do so within, or after, their freshmen year. College administrators believe that learning communities can help students stay in school by providing opportunities for students to become more connected to the college.

Nearly all of the studies on the impact of learning communities show that students who participate are more likely to stay in school beyond their freshman year. In one of the early studies on learning communities conducted at Stony Brook University, it was found that the retention rate for the general population was 55%. However, the students from the learning communities stayed in school at a rate of 95%! Although not all the results have been this dramatic, they have all demonstrated the success of learning communities on retention of sophomore students.

Increased retention rates have also been shown for under-prepared learners. These are students who could be strong in one area but weak in another, or students who need a great deal of work in the first semester to prepare them for college-level work. Learning communities specifically designed for these students offer many of their needed classes, as well as tutors and advisors, mainly for the program participants. A high rate of under-prepared students complete these programs and go on to be successful in the classroom for the remainder of their college career.

■ INCREASED SOCIAL INTERACTION AND CAMPUS INVOLVEMENT

It can be argued that the primary reason for the increased retention rate is the effectiveness of learning communities in helping students feel connected to the school. Learning communities provide a venue for students to interact with other students and with faculty members in small classrooms and in informal settings. This interaction is so important. In the typical college, particularly in the first-year classroom, students passively receive material and demonstrate learning through tests and papers. Although this is an extreme example, it is likely that a first-year student can attend a semester's worth of college classes without interacting with any classmates or the professor. This is much less likely to happen in a learning community where classes are small and activities are provided away from the typical classroom setting, which encourages interaction. Even in learning communities where students take most of their classes with non-participating students, the participants spend so much time together that it would be difficult to not interact at all.

You have seen examples of how learning communities help students become more connected to the school. Students who participate have more interaction with faculty members and other students, and are more involved on campus. This promotes campus connectedness, which is also a major factor in student retention.

Participating students hear about activities from their peers or the peer leader in their community. Students are talking to faculty members more, so they are more aware of the campus and its resources. Students are also more comfortable with the campus because of the supportive peer relationships that they form in the community. Thus, participating students feel more confident in seeking out the activities on campus that they are interested in.

■ STRONGER INTELLECTUAL DEVELOPMENT

Research has shown that students who participate in learning communities demonstrate stronger intellectual development. Learning community participants from all types of schools have shown a level of intellectual development that is generally found only at small elite colleges.

At Daytona Beach Community College, students wrote three essays over the course of their freshmen year. The essay topics were on decision making, career plans, and learning in the classroom. The researchers used the Cognitive Development model and compared the learning community students to national data on freshmen. They found that students in learning communities progressed intellectually at a much greater rate than the national norm. The strong intellectual development found in these studies may be the most important impact of learning communities.

The main goal of college is to discipline the students' mind so they become lifelong critical thinkers and effective problem solvers. It stands to reason that students who are challenged to connect their course material together in new ways would have stronger intellectual development than students who view their course work as isolated areas. If you are able to look at history not just as history but how it relates to sociology, psychology, and culture, your mind is trained in new ways and you learn to view problems in a larger context. This may be why the strongest impact on intellectual development is in the team-taught programs.

The increased intellectual development allows the learning community student to demonstrate more intellectual maturity than other students. Learning community students are able to understand that they are ultimately responsible for their own education. This leads to their increased retention and could be one of the reasons they graduate at a higher rate. If students know that they are responsible for their own learning they are likely to work harder and be knowledgeable about course requirements for graduation. They may also be more in tune with their skill areas, which is helpful when choosing a major.

■ INCREASED STUDENT SATISFACTION WITH COLLEGE

In addition to the benefits just discussed, researchers found that learning community students are happier with their overall school experience as students and as alumni. Perhaps it cannot be directly attributed to their learning community experience. However, the learning community experience encourages the student to stay in school and to get involved academically and socially. These connections encourage further involvement throughout the years and often lead to deeper friendships, longer-lasting relationships with faculty, and meaningful experiences as student leaders. Perhaps those later experiences contribute more toward student satisfaction than the original learning community experience. However, there are two things to consider. When asked about their learning community and overall college experience, alumni often fondly recall their learning community experience and give specific examples of why it was important to them. Also, if the learning community initiates a chain of events that ends in a successful and satisfying college career, then it certainly meets many of its intended goals.

The next section describes a few of the most common types/models of learning communities. Find out if your campus has these types of learning communities, or something similar, available to you.

FINDING YOUR PLACE ON CAMPUS

The Washington Center for the Improvement of Undergraduate Education reports that every type of college/university in America offers learning communities to at least 10% of their student body. Some schools even report that they are offering learning communities to 90% of their undergraduate students.[5] This means that whether you are at a research university, a liberal arts college, or a community college you are likely to find some type of learning community that suits your needs.

To be effective, a learning community should have a specific purpose—perhaps to provide a greater sense of community for the participants, or to provide extra assistance to students who are under-prepared for college. The communities should be smaller than other units on campus. They should also help the faculty members feel more connected to the students in their courses, as well as to other faculty members.

There are hundreds of learning community programs offered across the country. They center on four basic models:

♦ **Student Cohorts/Integrative Seminar**

♦ **Linked Courses/Course Clusters**

♦ **Coordinated Studies**

♦ **Living Learning Communities**

---

[5]http://www.evergreen.edu/washcenter/home.asp

■ STUDENT COHORTS/ INTEGRATIVE SEMINAR

Twenty-nine percent of schools with learning communities describe their programs as *Student Cohorts/Integrative Seminar*.[6] In this model, a small group of students take a cluster of classes based on an area of interest, a topic, or a major. The group is called a *cohort* because the students take the classes, typically two to three, together. Although they are not the only students in those classes, all the cohort students take the same classes at the same time.

Additionally, the students take a seminar course called an *integrative seminar*. Typically they are the only students in the seminar course, which provides a method for the students to discuss how the other courses they are taking relate to one another. In this model it is assumed that the students in the community will seek each other out in their larger classes, and find friends and study partners without the aid of faculty members. This type of learning community is especially effective in creating smaller communities within a large college setting.

Student Cohorts at a Four-Year College

Originally implemented at the University of Washington, *Freshman Interest Groups*, or *FIGs,* is a popular example of student cohort/integrative seminar learning communities. Florida State University—a four-year, public, graduate, research university—offers Freshman Interest Groups to first-time college students in "an attempt to foster inquisitive thought and develop the mind as an instrument of analysis." At Florida State, FIGs are open to all incoming, first-time college students. However, students participating in other learning communities are not encouraged to join. Students learn about FIGs through a brochure sent to their home, through preview and their university orientation program, and through their academic advisor.

A FIG is a pre-packaged cluster of high-demand courses that fulfill general education requirements. At Florida State one advantage is that FIG students can enroll in higher level classes, which they normally have to take as upperclassmen because of the high demand, during the first semester of their first year. The program helps the community to form and grow because students choose a FIG based on an area of interest, groups are limited to 20–25 students, and includes a

---

[6]Learning Communities National Resource Center,
http://www.evergreen.edu/washcenter/project.asp?pid=73

weekly colloquium designed to help students reflect on their in-class and out-of-class learning experiences. In Fall 2005, students typically enrolled in 10 credits as a cohort: three 3-credit courses and the FIG colloquium. There are many different themes for FIGs: some are based on the students' intended major; others on more general areas of interest. Some of the FIG offerings in Fall 2005 included Diversity, America, Early Civilizations, Exercise Science, and Exploring Social Science.

In the Exercise Science FIG, one of the most popular, students take the following courses: Family Relationship Life Development (3 credits), Science of Nutrition (3 credits), Personal Fitness (3 credits), and the FIG colloquium (1 credit). The FIG colloquium includes a visit from at least one faculty member, who is encouraged to talk about his/her own work and expectations for undergraduate students.

A Freshmen Interest Group leader (FIG leader) is assigned to each group. The FIG leader is carefully chosen. To be considered, students must first be nominated by a faculty member. The students then complete an application that includes two additional references from faculty members. Applicants must have earned a 3.25 minimum GPA and 45 credit hours at the time they apply. FIG leaders are junior and senior students who have proven to be academically successful. As part of their training, all FIG leaders participate in a 1-credit course to gain the "knowledge, skills, and perspectives necessary to be a FIG leader." The course is taught by the Dean of Undergraduate Studies. Students learn about intellectual engagement, liberal studies philosophy, and teaching strategies. They then design and teach the colloquium class, under the supervision of a senior faculty member, and provide out-of-class support for the FIG participants, including advice on ways to get involved on campus, tips on studying, and how to best navigate campus.

Student Cohorts at a Community College

The University of Wisconsin at Marshfield/Wood County is a public school for first- and second-year students. In Fall 2005 they began offering a student cohort learning community for their first-year students. Administrators at UW-Marshfield/Wood County believe that their program helps tie their first-year seminar course to content areas and helps students connect better with faculty. The program provides intellectually-engaging work and a quality experience for first-year college students.

The faculty works together to design the program, but work independently in planning their syllabi and/or course assignments. As part of the overall theme all participants receive a copy of the book, *Affluenza,* and read and discuss it as a part of their seminar course.

These cohorts are open to all first-year students: participants take three classes together, including the First Year Seminar, based on a theme. As in other learning communities, the small class size is limited to no more than 22 students. During summer advising and registration sessions, students are told about the learning community; interested students then sign up for the program and register for all three courses. In Fall 2005 the school offered three clusters: Business and Ethics, Nature in Crisis, and the U.S. Constitution. In the Business and Ethics Cohort, students take Public Speaking, Introduction to Business, and First Year Seminar. As in many other student cohort learning communities, the seminar topic centers on the theme of the community—in this case, business ethics.

■ LINKED COURSES/COURSE CLUSTERS

The *Linked Courses* and *Course Clusters models* are the most popular types of learning communities. Fifty-nine percent of schools with learning communities classify their programs as either linked courses or course clusters.[7] These models require more faculty participation in the community than the student cohorts model. Although the faculty members in these courses do not often team-teach, they work together to design a comprehensive plan for the students. The primary difference between the two models is this collaboration. In student cohorts, faculty members do not need to coordinate any part of their curriculum; in linked courses or course clusters, the instructors collaborate in order to integrate the course material.

In the *linked courses model,* students register for two courses that are linked thematically or by content. The faculty members coordinate their syllabi for the two courses but teach each course separately. Examples of paired courses are Technical Writing and Introduction to Environmental Science, and Introduction to Public Speaking and American History. Outside a learning community, it may seem that these courses have no relation to one another. However, faculty who teach in the learning community work together outside the classroom to ensure that the material they teach helps the students make the connection between the courses. As in student cohorts, the goal is not only to create community but also to improve critical thinking and writing through that community.

---

[7]Learning Communities National Resource Center,
http://www.evergreen.edu/washcenter/project.asp?pid=73

Course clusters are very much like linked courses but include more than two courses. A participant's course schedule may include English, Writing, Philosophy, Art, and a one-credit course designed to help the student integrate what is happening in each of the other four courses. Faculty who teach courses in this learning community review syllabi and course evaluations from previous years, share themes and course objectives, and consult one another on the textbook that they use. This type of learning community requires more faculty involvement than the student cohort model, but less faculty involvement than the coordinated study model (which will be discussed on pages 29–30).

Linked Courses/Course Clusters at a Four-Year College

In the College of Liberal Arts and Sciences at Arizona State University, first-year and continuing students can participate in a learning community with or without a residential component. The learning communities are small and limited to a maximum of 100 students. These allow the participants to connect with their peers and the faculty in a way that they normally wouldn't at this large, research-based university.

The communities are built on themes. One of the themes for the Fall 2005 was Baseball Diamonds. Students enrolled in 12 credits, which included: *First Year Composition:* Baseball Fungoes; *Mathematics:* Math, Society, and Box Scores; *Comparative Sports and Culture:* Introduction to Serious Fun; and *Introduction to Ethnic Studies:* Baselines and Color Lines.

Don't be fooled by the sports theme—students are intellectually challenged in this program by some of Arizona State's most renowned faculty. They are chosen for their dedication to undergraduate teaching, each having received teaching awards, and are talented in the classroom. These veteran faculty members work together to create syllabi for the courses, collaborate on assignments, and sometimes teach together. The material in each course is based on what is covered in the other courses. Students in this baseball-themed community will learn to think critically about culture, socialization, race, and class, as well as integrate college-level writing and mathematics with the material that they receive in psychology and anthropology. In addition to teaching, faculty members socialize with the students over shared meals and community field trips.

Each learning community is assigned a university librarian, an undergraduate peer leader, and an academic advisor. This team provides students assistance with research, academics, and the social aspects of college life.

According to research completed on their own programs, student participants at Arizona State University develop greater research and writing skills than their peers who do not participate in a learning community.

Linked Courses/Course Clusters at a Community College

At Cerritos College, a community college in Norwalk, California, first-year students have had the opportunity to participate in learning communities since 1995. The learning communities at Cerritos, like many others, are intended to promote student success and to recognize the diverse needs of students. The First Year Experience learning community is intended to provide students with a strong beginning to their college career. The faculty who teach in the learning communities are involved with the students in and out of the classroom. They serve as the teacher and academic advisor, and they also conduct the college orientation for their students. The course instructors integrate their syllabi, encouraging students to understand their courses and discover how they relate to each other.

Students learn through classroom assignments, tests, field trips, research projects, and educational technology. Additionally, a retention counselor is available to the students. The retention counselor helps the students succeed by offering on-line and face-to-face counseling, as well as workshops on study skills. Students in the learning communities are offered tutoring, study groups, and social events, all of which promote their academic and social connectedness to the college.

Fifteen communities are offered to students each semester on a wide range of topics, including English, Anthropology, Physics, English as a Second Language, and Theater. The program is currently expanding and, in the future, may include Business and Vocational Studies. In the First Year Experience learning community, students take a full semester's worth of work in the community. They enroll in a learning community based on their level of aptitude: basic or intermediate skills, or transfer (those who wish to transfer to a four-year college). In the Basic Skills track students take English, English Lab, Reading, Contemporary Health Problems, and split the semester for nine weeks of Career Planning and nine weeks of Orientation and Educational Planning. Students who participate in the Intermediate Skills track take English and English Lab, Math, Physical Education, and Success for College and Career. Students in the learning communities must enroll in all of the learning community classes in order to participate.

■ COORDINATED STUDIES

In the *Coordinated Study model,* faculty members actually team-teach. This is a unique form of teaching and learning in the college setting. The students are immersed in the material that they are learning across disciplines; the faculty participates not just as teachers but as learners. Twenty-eight percent of schools with learning communities use the Coordinated Study model.[8]

In the team-taught course plan, there may be two courses taught by two teachers together. In this community, Introduction to Chemistry and Intermediate Algebra become "Chemath" and are taught in one class by two faculty members. In an even more involved structure, students take their full semester course load (15–18 credits) within the community. Learning is centered on themes. Faculty co-plan and co-teach these courses across disciplines. Because students only take courses within the community, and faculty teach only within the community, scheduling becomes quite flexible and allows for creative teaching that would not occur in a typical classroom. These programs may be the most effective in creating an interdisciplinary learning environment, which requires large amounts of student–faculty interaction, and produce unique and creative teaching methods that involve both the teachers and the students in the learning process.

Coordinated Studies at a Four-Year College

Proving that not all learning communities are for first-year students only, all sophomore students at Stonehill College participate in fully-integrated learning communities. Stonehill is a small, private Catholic college in Easton, Massachusetts. Its liberal arts curriculum is embedded in their Cornerstone Program, which aims to provide students with the tools to critically examine themselves and the world. Through the Cornerstone Program, first-year students take four courses: history, literature, philosophy, and religious studies. Building on the knowledge and skills gained in their first year, second-year students enroll in a coordinated study learning community that integrates disciplines to formulate a thorough understanding of a subject.

All students select three preferences for learning community topics—all of which include two classes from two different disciplines and an integrative seminar—and they are placed into one of their three choices. In 2004–2005, approximately 600 sophomores chose from 25 learning communities. One community offered in

---

[8] Learning Communities National Resource Center,
http://www.evergreen.edu/washcenter/project.asp?pid=73

2004 was entitled "Autobiography: A Verbal and Visual Exploration of Selfhood." Members in this community participated in three courses: Studio Arts 1; Mining the "I": Reading and Writing Autobiography; and Integrative Seminar. As described in their course catalog, this learning community explores the relationship between writing and visual arts. Students in this learning community take field trips, meet professional writers and artists, and work hands-on in the studio. Students keep a journal of their verbal and visual discoveries. Another learning community offered students the opportunity to travel to France as part of the integrative seminar to learn about "Art, Culture, and Literature in 19th Century France."

Stonehill College continues the Cornerstone program throughout the students' entire undergraduate career. It offers courses in moral reasoning for juniors, a capstone experience for seniors, and several requirements that can be taken any year, including those within a learning community.

Coordinated Studies at a Community College

At Daytona Beach Community College in Florida, first-year students have the opportunity to participate in a nationally-recognized learning community called *Quanta*. Quanta is a full-year program involving nine credits per semester. Like other successful learning communities, Quanta is small; it is limited to 66 students per semester. Students who choose to participate in the Quanta program register for a cluster of three courses—English, Humanities, and Psychology—all of which count toward their core course requirements for their Associate of Arts degree.

These courses are not taught separately, as in the general college classroom or in other types of learning communities. Instead, students in the Quanta program are in one classroom on Mondays, Wednesdays, and Fridays from 9 AM–12 noon with the three faculty members who team-teach the courses. This holistic learning experience centers on a theme. During fall semesters the theme is "The Quest for Identity: The search for Identity and Intimacy" and focuses on the human journey to discover self and its relation to others. In the spring semester Quanta students study based on the theme of "Values & Visions: Creating a Better World." Students who participate in the Quanta program are encouraged to register for only one course outside the program, typically a math class. Participating students are also encouraged to allow, in their schedule, one hour after each class for lunch and to socialize with the students and faculty in their community.

■ LIVING/LEARNING COMMUNITIES

Thirty-one percent of schools that offer learning communities indicate that their programs are *Living/Learning Communities.*[9] These programs involve students who live together in a particular area of a residence hall. The program has staff and resources, which are not available to other students, dedicated solely to that community. These communities are also based on different themes. Some communities are centered on the students' major; others on the students' desire for a certain lifestyle, such as health and wellness, or part of a desire to grow in a certain area, such as leadership development.

Living/learning communities are typically small with 50 or less students.[10] Most of the communities are selective. Students are chosen to participate based on their experiences in high school, grades, essay, or some other criteria. Students in the living/learning community participate in academic or co-curricular programs specifically designed for them. Some communities offer co-curricular programs outside the classroom without academic credit. Activities may include team-building, cultural outings, multicultural programs, community service, career workshops, and intramural sports, among others. Other communities offer special academic courses or special sections of larger introductory courses solely for their members. In addition to social and classroom functions, living/learning communities often offer academic advising and study groups for its participants.

Like other learning communities, these programs are found to be successful. Students who participate in these communities have positive interactions with their peers and have a smoother transition to campus. Students who participate in learning communities get more involved in academic and social activities on campus. By having a supportive network of their peers that reach outside the borders of the classroom, they are more likely to stay in school.

Sometimes when programs are created to help students succeed, students do not realize their benefits. However, we found that most students in living/learning communities are pleased and excited about their experience. Washington State University, where Freshmen Interest Groups were formed, gathered feedback on the program. Their research found that within the first two years of the program, both students and faculty felt that the programs should continue. They identified the benefits of the program as being great ways to make friends, helping them adjust to college life, and helping them develop a greater interest in their classes.

---

[9]Learning Communities National Resource Center,
http://www.evergreen.edu/washcenter/project.asp?pid=73

[10]The Residential Learning Communities International Clearinghouse,
http://www.bgsu.edu/colleges/as/pcc/resources2.html

Because of the component requiring students to live together in the same campus residence hall, living/learning communities are found on campuses that offer on-campus housing. Although some community colleges are seeking to expand their options for student living, including building on-campus residence halls, the majority do not include a residential component. However, within residential colleges the types of living/learning communities are as varied as the schools themselves.

Living/Learning Communities at a Four-Year College

Salisbury University, a midsize, public university in Salisbury, Maryland created the LEAD Scholars Program and offered it to incoming freshmen for the first time in Fall 2004. The LEAD Scholars Program targets students who have demonstrated leadership skills in high school and wish to become student leaders in college. It is designed to facilitate the growth of Salisbury freshmen into successful campus leaders. The program, a joint venture between the Leadership Center and the Office of Residential Life, is small by design. Salisbury offers spots in this living/learning community to 10 men and 10 women who are all in their first year.

Accepted students learn about the LEAD Scholars Program through information sent to their home from the Office of Residential Life. Interested students fill out an application, describe their leadership roles in high school and their strengths, and explain why they would like to be a part of the LEAD Scholars Program and why they should be chosen over their peers.

Students who participate in the LEAD Scholars Program live together in a campus Residence Hall. A Resident Assistant (RA) lives on the same floor as the students. This upperclass student advises the program participants on residential matters (much like other RAs), serves as a peer advisor to the students in the program, and often participates in the activities of the community.

Students in the LEAD Scholars Program participate in four primary community activities throughout their entire first year and earn one college credit for their efforts. The students attend weekly workshops on leadership in three levels—emerging, established, and experienced student leaders—taught by the Director of Student Activities, Organizations, and Leadership. Workshop topics include communication skills, time management, motivation, teamwork, values, multi-culturalism, and self-awareness.

The LEAD scholars also meet weekly to learn about various topics, including public speaking, networking, ethical decision making, and team building. During the fall semester, LEAD scholars participate in a community service project. In the spring semester they plan and implement a campus-wide program to benefit the students of Salisbury University. This final project is the culmination of the knowledge and experience gained by members of the LEAD Scholars community.

Table 1 shows the identifying characteristics of the four learning community models.

Table 1. Identifying characteristics of learning communities

Student Cohorts/Integrative Seminar	Linked Courses/Course Clusters
♦ Students take 3 or more courses together ♦ In most of their classes, learning community students are in the same class with other students ♦ All learning community students participate in one seminar course where they are the only students ♦ Instructors do not work together in the program but may meet with students out of class or participate in the seminar class	♦ Students take two or more clusters as a community, usually based on a theme ♦ Generally, the community students are the only students in the classroom ♦ Instructors collaborate on assignments and syllabi ♦ Grades may be given individually for each class or one grade is given for all classes ♦ Material form each course is related, in some way, to other courses offered in the community ♦ May or may not include an integrative seminar
Coordinated Studies	**Living/Learning Communities**
♦ Fully integrated program—students take between three classes to a full-semester load as part of the program ♦ Instructors plan and teach courses as a group ♦ Students attend classes in large chunks of time, rather than spending a specified time for each individual class	♦ Students live together in a residence hall on campus as part of the program ♦ Curriculum can contain parts of any of the other three community models

GETTING INVOLVED

Now you know what learning communities are, their goals, the benefits you can gain from them, and how much students enjoy being part of one. You may be wondering: "Is it too late for me to join a learning community and reap the benefits?" Although most learning community programs are geared toward first-year students, and this could be the case in your school, there are still many ways to get involved.

■ BE A PEER LEADER

Most learning communities have an upperclass student who helps out with the program. If the learning communities on your campus have peer leaders, see how you can become one. You may have to be nominated, apply, and interview for the position. As a peer leader you will have the same interaction with the students and faculty members as the learning community members. At the same time, you will be helping out first-year students.

As a peer leader you are a role model to the learning community members, provide tips on campus survival, and help students get involved. You also assist the faculty members in the program. You may even have the opportunity to teach classes. To become a peer leader it is important that you have a good academic record and are involved on campus. So be sure to keep your grades up and, if you haven't done so yet, check out the clubs and organizations on your campus. Generally peer leader positions are announced in your school paper or on the campus job board. However, don't wait to see the advertisements. Seek out information on peer leader positions now so that you will be ready to apply when the opportunity arises.

■ JOIN THE ADVISORY BOARD

Consider joining the learning community advisory board on your campus. It may be called something else on your campus, but the concept is the same regardless of its name. The advisory board is typically comprised of faculty, staff, and students. It meets periodically—from a few times a year to once each month—to determine the direction of the learning communities. Depending on the stage of the learning communities at your school, you may participate in training instructors or peer leaders, help evaluate current programs, or even create new communities.

A likely source of information on learning community advisory boards is your school's website. If the members are listed, you can contact the committee chair, or any of the members, to see how you can get involved. Typically, advisory boards are looking for more student input, so they will be eager to have you join. You can also seek information from your academic advisor or the person who teaches your First Year Experience Course. They are generally well-versed on what is available on campus. Other sources of information are the school newspaper, the Student Activities Office, the Learning Communities Office (if you have one), or the Residential Life Office.

■ CONDUCT A RESEARCH PROJECT

Another way of getting involved in learning communities is through research work. In the previous section, we learned how research studies have measured the impact of learning communities. The results of these studies show that learning communities are successful: participants feel more connected to the university, earn better grades, and get more involved on campus. However, there is always more research to be done.

If you are interested in research or if you plan on pursuing graduate studies some day (you need to have completed some independent research to be accepted to graduate school), you should consider doing an independent study to look into learning communities. You could study the impact of the learning communities at your college, possibly by looking at a specific program or group of students. For example, you may want to find out whether the students in the pre-med learning community were admitted to medical school at a greater rate than pre-med students who did not participate in the learning community. Generally, in order to complete an independent study, you would work with a professor for a semester or two and be rewarded academic credit for your work. The best way to look into an independent study on learning communities is to contact a faculty member in your learning communities' office. If your campus does not have an office or faculty members dedicated to learning communities, ask your academic advisor or a faculty member in your major how you can get involved in this type of independent study.

■ CHECK OUT LEARNING COMMUNITIES FOR UPPERCLASS STUDENTS

Don't assume that because you are now an upperclass student learning communities are no longer available for you. As learning communities become more successful, schools are expanding their programs beyond the first-year experience. Many schools are now offering learning communities to transfer students and all undergraduate students. Some schools are even offering learning communities to graduate students.

Learning Communities at Syracuse University

Syracuse University in New York has over 30 learning communities available to its students, many of which are open to all undergraduates. Syracuse has many options for students who live in the residence halls; many programs are also available for undergraduates who live off campus.

Like many other programs, new students learn of the communities before they begin school and can apply to the program. In the spring of each year continuing students can apply to up to three learning communities and are then placed in one of their three choices. All of the learning communities that are currently open to continuing students are the Living/Learning Programs. Interested students fill out an application, indicating which learning communities they are interested in.

Applicants answer these three questions:

1. Why do you want to become part of a learning community?
2. What do you hope to gain?
3. What do you have to offer?

Like many other programs, undergraduate students can select the learning community they want to join based on their major, area of interest, or a specific skill area.

Graduate Interest Groups

In addition to programs offered to new and continuing undergraduate students, Syracuse University is now offering learning communities to some of their graduate students. Similar to the Freshmen Interest Group model, these communities are called *Graduate Interest Groups* or *GIGs*. Syracuse chose to begin their first GIG in the Higher Education Administration graduate program. The Higher Education (HED) Graduate Interest Group is required of all matriculated first-year graduate students in their first semester. Much like a FIG, the HED's GIG is constructed so that students take courses with both members of their cohort and other masters and doctoral students. The cohort meets at scheduled times during the seminar to integrate material from the courses and to help new students transition into the graduate program.

Students who participated in the GIG program in Fall 2004 were really pleased with the connections it helped them make. Students noted that it helped them feel more comfortable with their new surroundings and meet more students and faculty. This goes to show that students of all ages and at all stages in their academic career can benefit from learning communities.

Find out if your school is offering learning communities to undergraduate students after their first semester in college. If they are, great! Find out how you can participate. If not, ask why. If enough students express an interest, your college may be willing to begin one.

PERSPECTIVES AND PROFILES

■ THE STUDENTS' PERSPECTIVE

We interviewed junior and senior students who had participated in learning communities about their experiences so we can better understand their benefits and challenges. Regardless of the type of learning community they participated in, students shared many of the same sentiments about their experiences.

What was memorable about the experience?

Students remember the strong bonds that they formed through the learning community. Some remember how strange they felt when they first met their roommate, particularly when they saw how different they were from each other. One student talked about how he saw his roommate, now one of his best friends, as being so different because he had a "funny" accent, and how his roommate's parents were also different. During the course of his experience he realized how inappropriate it was to make snap assumptions about someone. The learning community forced him to spend enough time with his roommate to really get to know him and challenge those false assumptions.

One of the many benefits of a learning community is that the small groups facilitate greater interaction within the community. This ultimately fosters a greater understanding of each other and allows them gain more from the range of experiences and backgrounds they are exposed to within the group. As with most college students, your preconceived notions and initial impressions about your peers often determine your attitude towards them. However, in a learning community, by spending more time with the members in your group you get to know them better. As you look back, you may find that your closest friends are those you initially thought were different from you.

The importance of becoming part of a community was a sentiment repeatedly echoed by students from learning communities. One junior student looks back at her learning community and realizes that her best friends came from that program. What she remembers most about the program was that it "really helped [her] to get to know people on a different level and create those important relationships." She also felt that the program helped her feel as though she was part of a smaller community, despite the fact that she was attending a large university. The small community allowed her to feel more at home, and gave her a sense of comfort that she may otherwise not have attained at this large institution. Learning communities create smaller communities within the college.

Most students are not as persuaded by research results as they are by the experiences they hear about from other students. Research results show that learning community students often stay in school and earn better grades. However, what could be most telling about the programs' success is the way the students feel about the program. The students we interviewed were thrilled with their learning community and the experiences it gave them. They repeatedly echoed the importance of the bonds they formed with other students and their fondness towards them. They felt that they had formed connections with students that they could not have formed in any other setting. They also learned about other campus activities and events through their learning community that non-participating students didn't know about. Many of the students also noted that they miss their community experience.

Did you have any negative experiences?

All the students we interviewed remember their experience as positive and were reluctant to talk about negative memories. However, they all cautioned participants about the dangers that can arise from a close-knit group. When students spend such a great deal of time together, disagreements and problems will inevitably arise. This is particularly difficult when it happens in living/learning communities because students often feel they never spend any time apart from one another. Stress and gossip become major factors, and small incidents quickly escalate into big issues. When this happens, it is particularly important that the issues be discussed and resolved immediately, or at least for the group to "agree to disagree," to maintain peace within the whole group. The undergraduate peer leader or the faculty advisors in the group are often very helpful in solving personal issues within the group because they are a neutral party.

What advice do you have for other students?

The strongest message from those who were in learning communities as first-year students is for participants to take advantage of this unique opportunity, which is not available to all students. Learning communities offer first-year students additional resources and relationships to be successful in their first year of college and beyond. Take advantage of this opportunity by opening your mind to new experiences. Look introspectively to understand who you are, and be brave enough to show your true self to the group. Just being part of a learning community is not necessarily a predictor of future success: the greater your involvement in the group, the greater your likelihood of benefiting from the overall experience. There are numerous people with different experiences to learn from in your community—your peers, the faculty, and the student leaders in your group—and it is your responsibility to do just that, *learn*.

Another advice: Open your mind to students who are different from you and learn from your faculty and your peers. Learning communities provide you the opportunity to be part of a close-knit but diverse group who will share the same experiences. Possibly for the first time in your life, you will be exposed to a group of people with different beliefs, backgrounds, and experiences, and it is your responsibility to learn from them as they can learn from you. Take time to learn from your mentors, peers, and faculty; you will learn not only from your classes but from each other. To quote one student: "Do not hesitate, drop all your barriers, and be willing to develop and grow with others." However, don't forget to be yourself. "People come in all shapes and sizes, with different ideas and philosophies; you cannot benefit from an experience if you are not honestly yourself in that experience."

STUDENT PROFILE:
KATIE RIORDAN

- ◆ **Sophomore at Salisbury University, Maryland**
- ◆ **Business Administration major; minor in Communications**
- ◆ **Participated in the LEAD Scholars Program**

> 1. *How did you become interested in the learning community that you participated in?*
>
> I developed an interest in the LEAD Scholars program when I received a pamphlet in the mail with a description of the program. It is a Living/Learning Community for students who are interested in leadership.

I knew I wanted to get involved in something when I got to Salisbury, but at the time I wasn't sure just what. I decided I had nothing to lose by filling out an application. Looking back, it was one of the best decisions I could have made for my college career.

2. How were you selected to join?

If you wanted to become a part of LEAD Scholars you had to fill out an online application. The application asked for information regarding high- school leadership experience, why you were interested in getting involved, and your favorite quote.

3. What did you think of it at the time?

When I first received the information packet about LEAD Scholars, it seemed like a great opportunity to get involved on campus in a positive way. Although I didn't know many specifics of the program, I knew I was a person who constantly assumed leadership positions. I was very excited about the possibility to become a part of something great.

4. Looking back, how has it impacted your college experience?

LEAD Scholars has opened the doors to so many opportunities for me. I was able to receive outstanding leadership training through a series of workshops and programs we participated in. Through LEAD Scholars I was introduced to Salisbury University's Residence Hall Association and became the Vice President of Public Relations. Also, I met people who were able to help me and my two friends establish the Women's Club Lacrosse Team, which did not previously exist here at Salisbury. Being a part of the program helped me develop confidence in my leadership abilities that I had never experienced before. I was always encouraged to do my best and push myself farther than I ever had. I have been hired to be a Resident Assistant for my sophomore year and I attribute much of that to my involvement with LEAD Scholars.

We were also encouraged to become peer leaders around campus, so I looked into it and am currently working with the university's new student orientation program and will be a student facilitator with the First Year Experience course in the fall. LEAD Scholars got me involved in the community as well through Habitat for Humanity, Relay for Life, the Big Event, and volunteer work at a local assisted-living home. Through LEAD Scholars I have made friends I will never forget and had experiences that have changed my life.

5. If you were to tell someone how you feel about your school, what would you say?

I absolutely love everything about Salisbury University. It is the perfect school for me. It's just the right size, the faculty and staff members are amazing, the people are more than friendly, and there's always something to get involved in. There are not enough words to describe how much I enjoy being a student here.

6. What do you remember about your experience?

My experience with LEAD Scholars was incredible and forced me to learn a lot about myself. I was able to discover what I really wanted from my college experience, and that allowed me to grow as an individual and as a leader. Although there were times when people disagreed on subjects, I feel the LEAD scholars were also able to grow as a group. Through this program students were able to make a difference in others' lives and that is something I will never forget.

7. What is the best advice you can give to a first-year student who is participating in a learning community?

Students need to be honest with themselves as to the reasons why they are taking part in their chosen living/learning communities. If you are involved in a program for the wrong reasons, you do not belong there and will be unhappy. Do not take part in a program because your mom or dad wanted you to, or because a friend is doing it. Only do the things that are going to make you happy, and allow and encourage you to grow.

8. What role did the faculty play in your learning community?

The Director of Student Activities and an undergraduate peer leader were in charge of the LEAD Scholars Program this past year. The peer leader played a major role in the different activities we did, such as Beyond the Limits—a ropes course to encourage team building and promote leadership—and also in our community service events, such as Habitat for Humanity and Relay for Life. The Director of Student Activities was in charge of running our leadership workshop series each semester. If we had any questions or ever needed any help, they were always there for us. They were amazing facilitators of the program and also led by example. They are the two women I look up to on this campus and I am thankful everyday for the opportunities they have given me throughout the past year. The LEAD Scholars Program is very lucky to have such great role models for the participating students.

9. Anything else you would like to say to first-year students?

Seize every opportunity to get involved in something you enjoy. Keep in mind that you are in college first and foremost for an education, but don't ever forget to have fun. Take advantage of the resources provided for you and never hesitate to ask for help. Always follow your heart and never give up on your dreams.

STUDENT PROFILE:
LAUREN THOMAS

- ♦ *Senior at Florida State University, Tallahassee*
- ♦ *Communications major; minor in Business*
- ♦ *Participated in a living/learning community focusing on academic subjects*

1. How did you become interested in the learning community that you participated in?

I first learned about the learning community from FSU's website. I was interested in it because it focused on political science. I was really interested in learning more about that area and meeting students that had the same interests as me.

2. How were you selected to join?

There was an application process where I had to fill out a basic application and then write two essays. The faculty involved in the program read the essays and made the selections.

3. What did you think of it at the time?

I absolutely loved my learning community and made friends that I am still close to today. I had the best experience and actually still say today that I wish I could live in the residence hall again.

4. Looking back, how has it impacted your college experience?

I feel that my learning community experience has certainly added to my college experience. The learning community allowed me to meet a diverse and involved group of students that, therefore, have allowed me to get involved in many areas on campus that I wouldn't have otherwise. This also has made some great contacts for me around campus and really added to my college experience as a whole. The learning community also allowed me to make some wonderful friends that I would not have made without it. I loved my learning community! I'm very involved on campus: with my sorority, through University Orientation, Student Alumni Association, Peer Leader for First Year Experience Course, Dance Marathon, Homecoming, Student Judicial Board, and FSU College of Democrats.

5. *If you were to tell someone how you feel about your school, what would you say?*

I would say that this is the best university in the U.S.A. We have a wonderfully diverse and energized student body that does so much for the surrounding community. College has something for everyone and if you are willing to put yourself out there and try something new, you will be amazed at not only the people you meet, but all that you will learn from doing so. I love it here!

6. *What do you remember now about your experience?*

I remember the people and the challenges I faced as a new student. The learning community helped shrink FSU for me and allowed me to try new things and get involved on campus.

7. *What is the best advice you can give to a first-year student who is participating in a learning community?*

I would say to be daring and try new things. You will be amazed at what you can learn from such a great group of students that are going through all of the same things that you are going through as a new student. Also get involved around campus, and bring a friend with you if you are scared about getting involved. You make your college experience and it will be all that you make of it.

8. *What role did the faculty play in your learning community?*

I remember that the professor I had for one of the required classes really challenged us, really made us feel as if we were in college, and that we had the ability to change the world if we wanted. He was wonderful. However, the faculty were not as involved as I thought they would be; mostly just in the colloquium.

9. *Anything else you would like to say to first-year students?*

Make the most of your time in college because it will fly by and you never want to look back and say that you wish you would have done more. Also have no regrets about college, experience and learn all that you can in the four years you have because they will be over before you know it.

EDDIE STANKIEWICZ

- *Senior at Florida International University (FIU)*
- *Marketing Major*
- *Participated in a Freshmen Interest Group (FIG) during his first semester of college*

1. How did you become interested in the learning community that you participated in?

My learning community was a Freshmen Interest Group (FIG). It consisted of a couple of classes and a First Year Experience Course. I chose the FIG because I attended a late orientation program and it seemed like the easiest way to get a good schedule. The FIG communities offered a pre-made schedule.

2. How were you chosen to participate?

I signed up through academic advising at orientation. I told my academic advisor that I was interested in the FIG and was able to sign up.

3. What did you think of it at the time?

I liked it because it was a good schedule for my first semester, but it ended up being a better experience than I thought it would be. I went to a smaller high school and FIU is huge. The FIG took away my fear of the university's size and made it smaller. I really appreciated the community and also the academic help. I pledged a fraternity that semester and found out that my pledge brothers were having a hard time with the same classes that I was doing well in, and these were smart guys. I ended up with the highest grade point average in my pledge class. I think this was because we (the students in the FIG) would get together and help each other at lunch, and because the professors were open to meeting with students outside their office hours.

4. Looking back, how has it impacted your college experience?

We really helped each other with classes and with meeting people. It was a growing experience for me and I made some real connections. Last year I went to a birthday party for someone who was in my FIG. Almost everyone from the FIG came to the party; it is amazing that so many of us have kept in contact. Everyone said that their grade point average is over 3.0.

When I came to FIU as a commuter student I never thought that I would get involved on campus. Now I am a huge school supporter. I am very involved in my fraternity, serving in various leadership roles and have served on the governing council for all the fraternities on campus. I helped form a business fraternity so that I could become more involved in my major. I had a role in Student Government and am even running for Homecoming King. This year I am an orientation leader/peer advisor. My FIG provided me with the opportunities to get involved and to meet people that I never would have met.

5. If you were to tell someone how you feel about your school, what would you say?

I love it. I am a strong school supporter, having found lots of ways to get involved on campus—even as a commuter student. There is something for everyone at FIU.

6. What is the best advice you can give to a first-year student who is participating in a learning community?

FIGs are great because they put together a great schedule for you. The times are well-balanced and the coursework is a good mix for a first-year student. The professors have experience really working with students, not just lecturing, and they can be mentors. Don't be afraid to ask questions; talk to your classmates and the professor. You can learn a lot from other students and you can help each other do better.

7. What role did the faculty play in your learning community?

The Director of Campus Life at FIU was the instructor for our First Year Experience Course. He is really the person who got me involved on campus. He reached out to me and opened doors. I think he took a special interest in me because I was pledging a fraternity and he understood what that was like. I really appreciate his efforts; you could tell he really cared about us.

■ THE PROFESSORS' PERSPECTIVE

Teaching in a learning community can be challenging. It can be somewhat difficult to collaborate with other faculty members when creating syllabi for coursework and coordinating assignments. In addition to the time faculty typically commit to coursework—for lesson plans, grading, office hours, and teaching—those who choose to teach in a learning community may have to commit extra time meeting with the community instruction team to coordinate lesson plans, as well as participating in social activities within the community. Learning community professors are not generally paid any additional money, so you may wonder why they choose to participate. You may also wonder why they continue to teach year after year. You can definitely benefit from their advice on what to do, and not to do, when participating in a learning community.

Why teach in a learning community?

The professors interviewed for this survey are all currently connected to a learning community in some way, either through teaching or program administration. All were very passionate about learning communities, believing that there are great benefits for students who participate and who take advantage of what communities have to offer. They started teaching in a learning community out of curiosity—to see what a unique classroom concept would do to college teaching. They also became involved for many of the same reasons that learning communities are started on campus, which included a desire to improve learning in the classroom and create stronger communities for students.

Echoing the thoughts of others, one professor said:

> As a faculty member, I wanted to have closer contact with the students, to create a classroom atmosphere where students and teachers could work together, where the old barriers could be broken down a bit, where the 'sage on the stage' was no longer there, to decentralize the classroom and make it more democratic.

Like many others, she continued to teach in the program because she saw these goals realized, and had fun in the process.

Professors who teach in learning communities find their students more engaged in the learning process, more prepared for class, and participate more inside the classroom than students in traditional classrooms, which are rewarding for the teacher. They also enjoy collaborating with the faculty from other disciplines and recognize that they themselves are learning. When talking with these professors, you can tell that they are committed to students and to the student learning process. Their experiences with learning communities have allowed them to work with students who have been very successful, as well as those who have not been successful, in learning communities.

How can students be successful?

Faculty members who taught in learning communities had the opportunity to observe firsthand their impact on participants. Their success stories echo those in the literature: students who take advantage of the community are more deeply connected to the college and to their own learning experience, and they form strong bonds with their fellow community members. The keys to student success are taking advantage of the community, participating in classroom discussion, preparing for class, attending the optional events, and taking the time to talk with the faculty members and peer leaders in the community. Learning communities set the stage for student success; however, the student needs to put in the effort to make it work.

This leads to the discussion of how the faculty members have seen students join learning communities for the wrong reasons. They reported cases of students taking advantage of the system: for example applying to a community for the sole purpose of living in a particular residence hall. The professors didn't feel that these students set out to abuse the communities. However, these students didn't reap the benefits offered by learning communities. The nature of many learning communities allows for a great deal of group work. The teachers found that students who didn't learn to work with their group often dropped out of their programs, or didn't succeed in the way that others did. Similarly, students who enter a learning community thinking that it will be the easy way are often disappointed at the level of thinking required from them. Learning communities purposely create small classrooms, so it becomes very obvious when a student has not completed the assignments.

Learning communities seek to alter the mode of teaching/learning and are geared towards more interaction in the classroom. Therefore, students who expect the instructor to impart knowledge in the form of a lecture, and for the student to then give that information back through their answers to the test, find learning community classes difficult. Faculty members mentioned how they would challenge their students to think about the material presented in class and in their readings, integrate that material, form their opinion, and share it with the class. However, they noted that this type of learning is not for everyone, so it is important to recognize your learning style if you are thinking of joining a community.

One professor noted that, interestingly, they have at least one student every semester who doesn't take to the learning concept and does not complete the assignments. However, the student continues to show up for each class session, knowing that he/she will fail. Although the student does not gain the intellectual development that this setting fosters, and may ultimately need to leave school because of failing grades, he/she appears to benefit in other ways from the experience provided by the learning community.

EXERCISES

1. The impact of learning communities have been determined by many studies completed at individual campuses. Using your library's database, find one study that examines the impact of learning communities on participating students at a school like yours.

   ♦ Summarize the article and discuss whether you agree or disagree with what the researchers found.

   ♦ Do you think that the impact found in these studies would be the same if done at a school different than yours? Explain your answer.

2. One of the major goals of learning communities is to integrate coursework across disciplines. Write a one-page paper describing how any two courses you are taking this semester relate to one another

3. Interview a faculty member who teaches in a learning community on your campus. Ask the following questions.

   ♦ How would you describe the learning community where you teach?

   ♦ Why did you get involved in the community?

   ♦ How do you think students can be most successful in the program?

   ♦ How can a student get involved in a learning community after their first semester in college?

   Write a newspaper article based on your interview.

4. Interview a student currently participating in a learning community. Come up with three or four questions to find out about their experiences in the learning community. Share the information with your class in a three-minute speech.

5. Create a short survey (10 questions maximum) on student involvement or student satisfaction. Ask 40 students on your campus to complete the survey (20 students who participated in a learning community and 20 students who did not participate).

    Based on the results of your survey, are the students who participated in learning communities more involved on campus than those who did not participate? (Hint: Ask a faculty member in the statistics department to help you analyze your data.)

6. Interview three to five upperclass students on whether or not they would advise you to join a learning community.

7. If you are thinking of joining a learning community, it is important to know what type of learner you are to determine if the environment is good for you. Use the Internet to find a learning assessment tool. There are many assessment tools that you can use (e.g., Myers-Brigs, Strong, or Campbell), so find one that will give you a good picture of your learning style.

RESOURCES FOR INSTRUCTORS

All of the examples used in this chapter have a website dedicated to their learning communities on their homesite. You can check them out for more information, or have interested students explore them for further information.

1. The Residential Learning Communities International Clearinghouse has terrific information on living/learning communities. The site includes research and some great examples. It can be found at **http://www.bgsu.edu/colleges/as/pcc/resources2.html**.

2. For further research on learning communities see the Learning Communities Bibliography, available online at **www.evergreen.edu/ washcenter** or at **http://temple.edu/lc**.

3. The Washington Center for Improving the Quality of Undergraduate Education is a fantastic website containing information on all types of learning communities, including their rationale, research, and examples for all types of schools. It can be found at **www.evergreen.edu/washcenter.home.asp**.

If you are looking for more information on starting a learning community on your campus, there are a lot of books that you can check out. I found the book, *Creating learning communities: A practical guide to winning support, organizing for change, and implementing programs,* by Shapiro & Levine, particularly helpful.

Note: Every effort has been made to provide accurate and current Internet information in this booklet. However, the Internet and information on it are constantly changing, so it is inevitable that some of the Internet addresses listed in this text will change.

 # REFERENCES

Chickering, Arthur, & Gamson, Zelda. (Fall 1987). *Seven principles for good practice in higher education.* Washington Center News.

Hill, Patrick. *The rationale for learning communities.* Washington Center for Improving the Quality of Undergraduate Education. Speech given at the Inaugural Conference on Learning Communities of the Washington Center for Undergraduate Education.

McGregor, Jean. (Spring 1994). *Learning communities taking root.* Washington Center News.

Shapiro, N., & Levine, J. (1999). *Creating learning communities. A practical guide to winning support, organizing for change, and implementing programs.* San Francisco, CA: Jossey-Bass.

Tinto, V. (1975). Dropout from higher education: A theoretical synthesis of recent research. *Review of Educational Research, 45*(1), 89–125.

Tinto, V. (1993). *Leaving college: Rethinking the causes and cures of student attrition.* (2nd ed.) Chicago, IL: University of Chicago Press.

Websites

Arizona State University, College of Liberal Arts and Sciences Website. http://clas.asu.edu/students/learningcommunities/

Cerritos College Learning Community Website. http://www.cerritos.edu/lcp/

Learning Communities National Resource Center. http://www.evergreen.edu/washcenter/project.asp?pid=73

Stonehill College Website. www.Stonehill.edu

The Residential Learning Communities International Clearinghouse.
http://www.bgsu.edu/colleges/as/pcc/resources2.html

Washington Center for Improving the Quality of Undergraduate Education.
http://www.evergreen.edu/washcenter/home.asp